Here we all are,
spot us, if you can.

We are animals, you and me;

We belong in the trees, We belong in the seas,

We belong on this land – It belongs to you and me.

So come, delve into our sunny world

To meet and see.

1

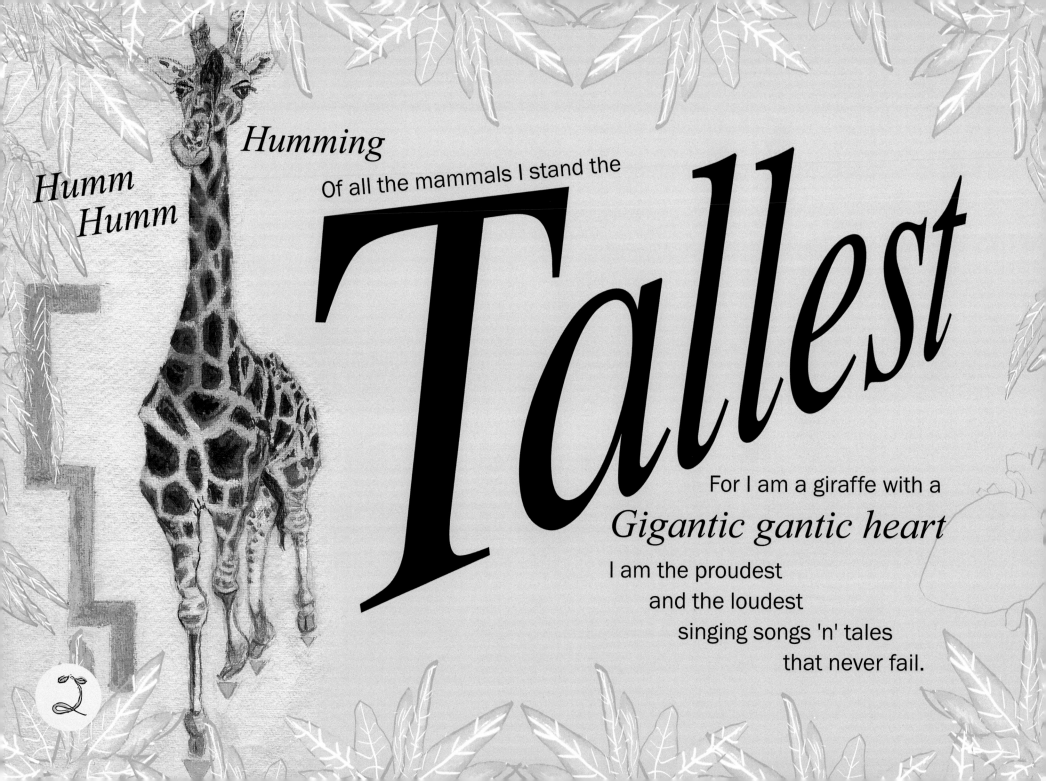

Humming

Humm
Humm

Of all the mammals I stand the

Tallest

For I am a giraffe with a

Gigantic gantic heart

I am the proudest
and the loudest
singing songs 'n' tales
that never fail.

"Ar____re?"

Buzz____ Bees

Cader Saul

More info contact: haffeera@gmail.com
Publisher: Independent Publishing Network
First paperback edition: June 2020
ISBN: 9781838535452
Illustrator & Author: Haffeera Cader Saul
Website: www.haffeera.com

Thank you to: you know who you are, especially
Mehr Gunawardina and Clare Bunnell Young
for helping editing and just being you

Where as I

Love

to wear and hide in my

stripy, stripe pinstripes.

They camouflage me well into the night,
causing hype. I snort with excitement and
Pure delight, causing a fright in our motion.
Dazzling coat, keeping me cool and the lions fooled.

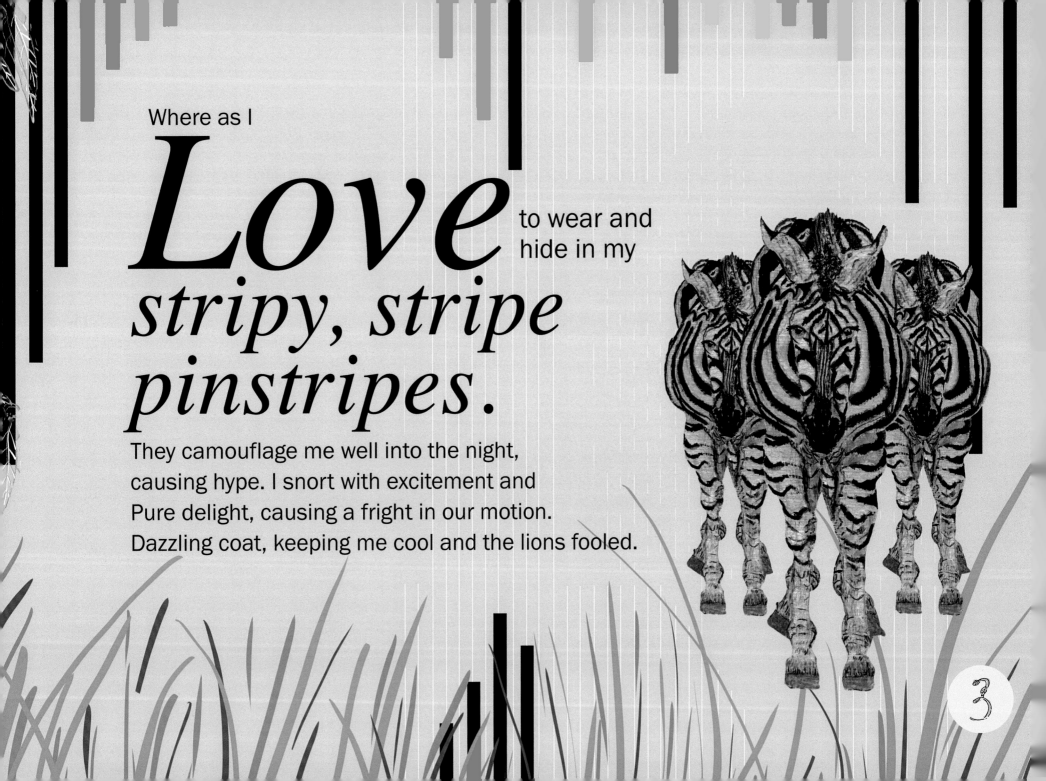

*I flew by the stripes
during my morning flight.
prrrp prrrpsss prrrp
prrrp prrrp prrrp*

prrrp prrrp

prrrp prrrp

Not a burp, but a purrp:
Blue-throated-bee-eater.
I fly low amongst the leaves,
below the palm trees,
before the rain to eat a few bees.

I meet and greet, quiver
my tail feathers as birds
of a feather we flock together,
no matter what the weather.
We glide and ride, being
the precious cargo on a Rhino.

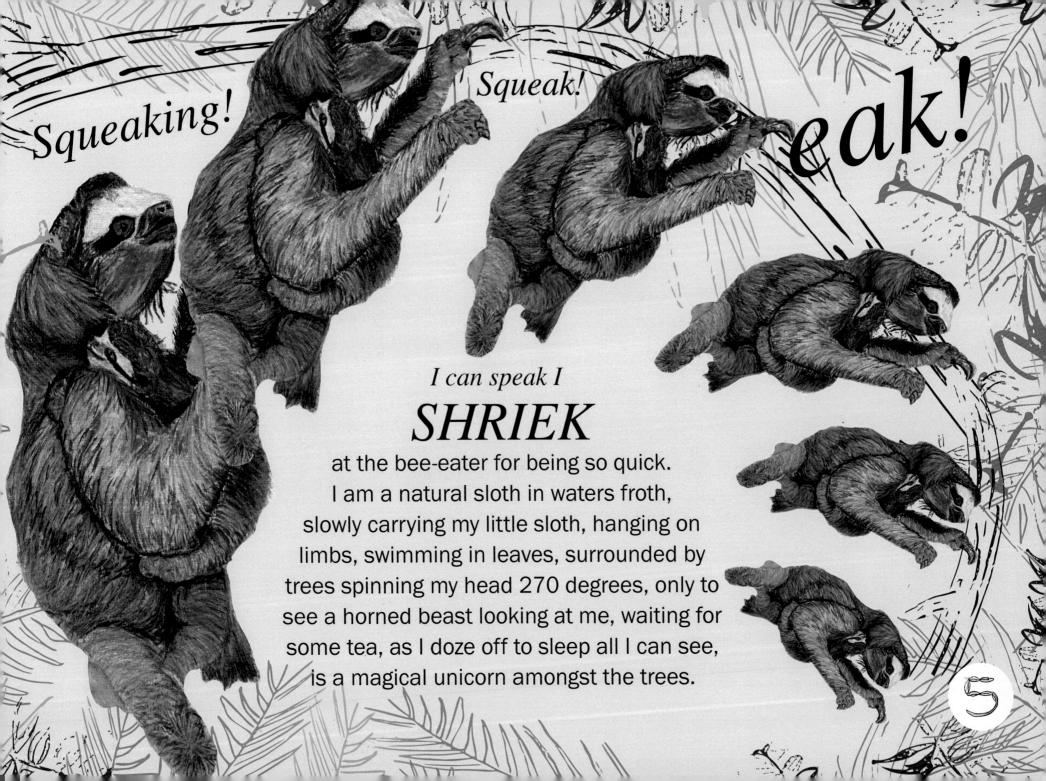

I can speak I

SHRIEK

at the bee-eater for being so quick.
I am a natural sloth in waters froth,
slowly carrying my little sloth, hanging on
limbs, swimming in leaves, surrounded by
trees spinning my head 270 degrees, only to
see a horned beast looking at me, waiting for
some tea, as I doze off to sleep all I can see,
is a magical unicorn amongst the trees.

I have a horn, but I am not a unicorn.

Nor is it made out of bone, it is not a cone. I have a weave that forms a keratin horn, that can grow and fall.

We rhinos are from worldly tribes who reside over tides, and take large strides from Africa to Asia.

My best friends will sit and ride to rest their feet before their next flight, taking a pew to Peru.

brrrrrrah
brrrrrrrrah

I, the humble, Humboldt Penguin,
love riding the sea,
in a wetsuit of feathers
in all types of weather
to visit the delicatessen
to feed my obsession.

I love to be free,
as I waddle from the Peruvian,
beautiful fishy sea, I become shy,
and hide using my darkness
and a branding of dots
for my future tots.

sssk

The humble, Humboldt penguin *loves* to *disguise* and we *love* to **hide**

Woof! Squawk! Eak!

We don't live on a prairie but we live in prairie dog town, buried **deep, deep down.** We bark sensing danger and squawk like a bird, when we want to talk.

Our vocabulary is **superior** to others, living with our families, greeting them with a kiss.

-x-

Here we all are,

We are all animals, you and me

We belong in the trees, We belong in the seas,

We belong on this land – It belongs to you and me.

As the animals explained to the bees.

Quiz

Have you been paying attention?
Here is a quick quiz to see.

Who has the biggest heart?

Who can turn heads 270^0?

What is a rhinos horn made of?

What animals did you see?

What animals wear pinstripes?

Did the animals meet the bees?

How many bees
can you find?